GW01260397

THE FOREST GARDEN
by Robert Hart

"Interesting ... packed with facts and information ... stimulates the imagination ... a complete contrast to the usual self-sufficient organic gardening book ... a true holistic approach to gardening" *Soil Association Review*

"A marvellous exposition of diversity and productivity and certainly the best I have seen about implementing the Agroforestry and Permaculture principles in the temperate conditions of Britain" *Permaculture News*

"It really sounds as though Robert Hart has established something very like the Garden of Eden" *Resurgence magazine*

As featured on the Channel 4 TV series 'Loads More Muck and Magic' and on Australian TV.

Fourth Edition 2001, £3-50 incl. p&p
Reprinted September 2003

The Institute for Social Inventions
6 Blackstock Mews
London N4 2BT
(tel 020 7359 8391; fax 020 7354 3831)

ISBN 0 948826 231

About the Author

Robert Hart's Forest Garden in Shropshire won one of the first awards for social innovation from the Institute for Social Inventions. This one-eighth of an acre model Forest Garden on his farm on Wenlock Edge, Church Stretton, was the first of its kind in England and the fruit of 30 years of study, research and practical experience in Agroforestry, a system of applied ecology developed by Hart.

A miniature reproduction of the self-maintaining eco-system of the natural forest, the Forest Garden fulfilled Hart's belief in the necessity of self-sufficiency. It was part of a larger consciousness of the inequalities between the Western and developing worlds and a desire to realise the infinite possibilities of a permaculture landscape, whereby aesthetic appeal was combined with conservation of the environment and the production of nourishing foods. In Kerala, he had observed how, despite a prodigious population density and considerable economic poverty, the state's 3.5 million forest gardens (the consequence of a land distribution initiative during the 1930s) guaranteed a high standard of living and a wealth of home-grown produce. It was a demonstration of how economic hardship and deprivation could be transcended by sustainability.

'Hart's own healing philosophy was consistently borne out in his life – and his garden'

Hart yearned for a Ghandian-based community. His Forest Garden perhaps represents a culmination of these values, at once self-sustaining, peaceful and symbiotic, and restorative of the harmony between man and the natural world; an area of beauty but also ecologic survival. Yet his vision, though wide-reaching, was resolutely practical: this book testifies to Hart's commitment to implementing the large-scale concepts of agroforestry practice in a manner appropriate to any sized garden. Now in its fourth edition, the book became an immediate bestseller with Ecologic Books, profoundly influencing the expansion of permaculture in Britain. It was later supplemented by the more comprehensive *Forest Gardening: Cultivating an Edible Landscape* and the *Forest Garden Video*.

Influenced as much by philosophers, artists and healers as by scientists, Hart's own healing philosophy was consistently borne out in his life – and his garden; an example of how a single person can positively effect change in their environment. His Forest Garden, likened to the Garden of Eden, attracted hundreds of pilgrims from all over England. He died peacefully on March 7th 2000, at a nursing home in Church Stretton, Shropshire.

The Forest Garden, *£3-50 incl. p&p from Insitute for Social Inventions (tel 020 7359 8391)*

Contents

Notes

If you start your own Forest Garden, please keep the Institute for Social Inventions informed, as your progress reports may be printed on the Global Ideas Bank (www.globalideasbank.org).

The Institute relies partly on sales of publications to help support its many charitable projects (including the Poetry Challenge, the Natural Death Centre, the ApprenticeMaster Alliance, www.DoBe.org and social invention workshops in schools) and would be very grateful for any reviews or mentions of this booklet that give the Institute's name and address (6 Blackstock Mews, London N4 2BT) and the price (£3-50 incl. p&p). There is a third off for orders of five or more.

Forest Garden was printed by Instant Print West One (tel 020 7434 2813).

6 Blackstock Mews, London N4 2BT, UK (rhino@dial.pipex.com), 2003, 27pp, ISBN 0 948826 23 1

Introduction

Behind my small stone farmhouse on Wenlock Edge in Shropshire is a miniature forest – only about one-eighth of an acre in extent. It is not there for ornament or to be coppiced for stakes or fuel, but to provide food and medicines, for it is the focal point of my self-sufficiency scheme.

'A multi-storey, self-regulating ecosystem that requires minimal maintenance'

It comprises some hundred different species and varieties of fruit and nut trees, fruit bushes and climbers, perennial, self-seeding and root vegetables and culinary and medicinal herbs, growing in the intensive conditions of the natural forest. Like the natural forest, it is a multi-storey, self-regulating ecosystem that requires minimal maintenance.

The storeys comprise tall fruit trees, constituting the **canopy**, nut trees and fruit trees on dwarfing rootstocks, constituting the **low tree layer**, currant and gooseberry bushes, constituting the **shrub layer** vegetables and herbs, constituting the **herbaceous layer**, dewberries and creeping herbs, constituting the **ground-cover layer**, root vegetables, occupying the 'rhizosphere', the **root layer**, and climbing berries and vines, constituting the **vertical layer**.

The system is self-perpetuating, because almost all the plants are perennial or active self-seeders such as borage and cress; self-fertilising, because deep-rooting trees, bushes and herbs draw upon minerals in the subsoil and make them available to their neighbours, and because the system includes both edible legumes which inject nitrogen into the soil, and mineral-rich plants such as buckwheat, which inject calcium.

'The trees are carefully selected to be mutually compatible or self-fertile'

It is self-watering, because deep-rooting plants tap the spring-veins in the subsoil, even at times of drought, and pump up water for the benefit of the whole system; self-mulching and self-weed-suppressing, because rapidly spreading herbs, such as mints and balm, soon cover all the ground between the trees and bushes and thus create a permanent 'living mulch'. It is self-pollinating, because the trees are carefully selected to be mutually compatible or self-fertile, and because the flowering herbs attract pollinating insects; self-healing, because the scheme includes a number of aromatic herbs, which undoubtedly deter pests and disease germs and exhale healing radiations. It is resistant to disease and pests also because any complex comprising a wide spectrum of different plants does not allow the build-up of epidemics such as affects monocultures.

This Forest Garden model, which could be reproduced even in smaller areas and in town gardens and wastelands, could, when well established, enable a family to enjoy a considerable degree of self-sufficiency for some seven months in the year, in the very best foods for building up positive health.

How it Started

It started with John Seymour, the well-known writer, broadcaster and organic pioneer, famed as the 'Guru of Self-Sufficiency'. Listening to a series of BBC talks in which he described how he and his wife Sally carved a miniature organic farm out of five acres of remote Suffolk heathland, I was badly bitten by the self-sufficiency bug.

'The garden – a model of a new civilised order, freed from the aberrations which lead to war'

A still more powerful influence on my organic development was the country writer H. J. Massingham, whose prolific works are now enjoying revived interest. Following a near-fatal accident which led to him losing a leg and the use of an arm, he found solace and salvation during the Second World War by building up a garden behind his cottage in North Buckinghamshire, dedicated to self-sufficiency and wholeness of living. Described in his masterpiece, *This Plot of Earth*, he regarded the garden as a model of a new civilised order, freed from the aberrations which lead to war and the destruction of the environment. Covering just one acre, the garden was an ordered jungle comprising a bewildering variety of fruit trees and bushes, vegetables, herbs and even two cereals – oats and maize – all interspersed with flowers and organically cultivated. Enjoying meals of home-grown produce throughout the year and mentally nourished by the ever-changing beauty of his environment, Massingham cured himself of chronic ailments, such as catarrh, which had formerly afflicted him, and found himself able to do twice the amount of intellectual labour he had done before his accident.

After searching far and wide, I was lucky enough to come across a beautiful old farmhouse, built of local red sandstone, in the hills of West Somerset. The land consisted of a steep five-acre pasture field and three acres of fruit, mainly blackcurrants, raspberries, apples and plums.

Having let the field to a local farmer, I proceeded to concentrate on working the fruit area on organic lines. The first thing I did was to build 17 compost heaps at strategic points, supplementing the numerous weeds which infested the fruit beds with cattle dung, straw, lime and seaweed which I culled from Dunster Beach. The largest heap I named 'Dungery Beacon' after Dunkery Beacon, the highest point of nearby Exmoor.

6 Blackstock Mews, London N4 2BT, UK (rhino@dial.pipex.com), 2003, 27pp, ISBN 0 948826 23 1

My tutor in beekeeping was a member of that rarest of species, the true English peasant. He was an indomitably cheerful little man who drove a horse-drawn cart and led an arduous life cultivating three and a half acres of precipitous terraced hillside, every square inch of which was covered with a wide variety of fruit, vegetables and fodder-crops, providing sustenance for himself, his wife and a flock of goats. I couldn't have had a better introduction to traditional self-sufficiency.

'Every square inch of land was covered with fruit, vegetables and fodder-crops'

After the Somerset experience I moved north to my present 20-acre farm on the NW slope of Wenlock Edge, a well-wooded limestone ridge which runs across the south of Shropshire. The small farmhouse, built of stone from a quarry in a wood on Roman Bank, as the hillside is called, stands by a spring which once supplied water for the whole neighbourhood. It occupies what is obviously a very ancient inhabited site at the junction of three causeways: a prehistoric track leading to a packhorse bridge through a hollow-way which at places is 40 feet deep; a Roman road leading to a quarry in Corvedale which supplied roofing tiles for Viroconium, and a track leading to a remote hamlet called Middlehope, which once boasted a Norman castle.

A horticultural adviser from the Ministry of Agriculture, who came to advise me about planting my first fruit trees and bushes, noticed a circular earthwork in the paddock above the house, and remarked, "This place shows the outline of a motte-and-bailey." This is a kind of fortification erected by the Normans of which many remains can be seen in this much-fought-over Welsh Border country. The motte is a circular mound which was surmounted by a wooden keep and the bailey a rectangular enclosure, originally stockaded, adjacent to it. An archaeologist who visited the site more recently believed, however, that the earthwork was the site of a Celtic monastery, while a depression to the south of the bailey, he suggested, may have been a monastic fishpond.

'All I did was to cover the garden with straw or compost when the plants died down in winter'

While my main enterprise was cattle rearing, I planted an orchard of apples and plums, and made the bailey, to the side and back of the house, the main focus for my horticultural activities. These comprised a large vegetable garden, a small orchard of apples and pears, a blackcurrant plantation and a garden of herbs and perennial vegetables, which meant digging up the lawn.

Over the years I found that this small garden, which included lovage, balm, applemint, eau-de-cologne mint, peppermint, dwarf comfrey, sweet cicely, sorrel, wild garlic and Good King Henry, was amazingly productive and trouble-free. It literally looked after itself. All I did was to cover it with straw or compost when the plants died down in the winter. Every spring they faithfully reappeared, sending out fresh shoots and leaves for months on end, thus providing us with the bulk of the green component of our diet for some five months. Pests and diseases were conspicuous by their absence.

I also experimented with companion planting of herbs in the vegetable garden. My first introduction to this ancient system was on my Somerset holding, where I found that plums had been interplanted with blackcurrants, a traditional association, as each set of fruit is believed to stimulate the other and possibly ward off each other's pests and diseases.

'Lavender is believed to ward off harmful insects from itself and neighbouring plants'

Blackcurrants are highly aromatic, as are most of the herbs and vegetables which are most prominent in companion planting lore. Just as lavender is used to deter moths in wardrobes, so it is also believed to ward off harmful insects from itself and neighbouring plants. The most generally practised form of companion planting in vegetable gardens is the growing of carrots and onions in adjacent rows, as the carrots are believed to ward off the onion fly and onion the carrot fly.

Among the herbs which I planted in my vegetable garden were applemint and borage. Borage, though an annual, is an avid self-seeder, and, by the second year, its sky-blue flowers had sprung up throughout the garden, so brilliant that a sort of electric haze seemed to hover above it. And the vegetables seemed to like it. Some that were almost throttled by borage nevertheless reached average size while the majority were healthy and free from pests and diseases.

'The herbs and perennial vegetables were quite happy to look after themselves'

In comparing the vegetable garden with the garden of perennial vegetables and herbs, it was obvious which demanded the least work. While the cultivation of conventional vegetables involved the arduous and fiddlesome annual chores of digging, raking, preparing seedbeds, sowing, transplanting, thinning out, hoeing, weeding, watering and composting, the herbs and perennial vegetables were quite happy to look after themselves. They needed little or no watering or composting, because their deep roots drew up water and minerals from the subsoil, for the benefit of themselves and each other, and they didn't even need weeding and hoeing, as they quickly spread over the whole surface of the soil, suppressing all competitors, while their intricate tangle of roots maintained a porous soil-structure. All they did need was

6 Blackstock Mews, London N4 2BT, UK (rhino@dial.pipex.com), 2003, 27pp, ISBN 0 948826 23 1

periodical thinning-out, to prevent them encroaching on each other, but, as they constituted an important part of our daily diet, a fair proportion of the thinnings found their way into the salad bowl.

Pondering on the contrast between the two gardens, it came to me that, if one could devise a diet consisting mainly of perennial vegetables, herbs, fruit and nuts, the task of achieving self-sufficiency would be vastly simplified. How this diet was worked out, with help from the writings of the famous Swiss pioneer nutritionist Bircher-Benner and the 17th century horticulturalist John Evelyn, will be described in the last chapter.

'A diet consisting mainly of perennial vegetables, herbs, fruit and nuts'

While I was writing my first book, *The Inviolable Hills*, Eve Balfour (then secretary of the Soil Association, who wrote the preface) sent me an article on Forest Farming by James Sholto Douglas. Pondering on how the system could be applied to temperate areas in the light of my own experience of growing fruit, perennial vegetables and herbs, and experimenting with companion planting, I worked out a system of applied ecology which came to be called Agroforestry. Later I found that others were working on similar lines in other parts of the world. I was particularly struck by a scheme that had been launched in the rainforest of South China. It comprised a multi-storey plantation of cardamom, cinnamon, cacao, cassia and rubber trees, interplanted with tea and coffee bushes, which received no irrigation, fertilisation, spraying or cultivations. After ten years it was stated to have achieved far higher yields than would have been possible under monocultural conditions. This success was attributed to the fact that the species of tree and bush had been carefully selected for ecological affinities between them, which enabled them to stimulate each other's growth, exchange nutrients, neutralise disease germs, ward off pests and circulate ground-water.

'Agroforestry has been practised for hundreds of years by peasant communities'

I also discovered that forms of agroforestry had been practised for hundreds or even thousands of years by peasant communities in many parts of the world, from East Africa, the supposed Cradle of Mankind – site of the 'Garden of Eden' – to Mexico and Central America, whose Indians have a vast secret herbal lore. A contributor to 'Mother Earth', the then title of the journal of the Soil Association, for April 1957, wrote: "Mexico is the pattern of ecology, and so, in spite of all her natural shortcomings, can teach us a lot .... The 'Indios' knowledge and practice of plant associations goes much further than ours, which is by comparison elementary. Their 'huertos' ('orchards') are mostly round the houses .... They are amazing shambles of banana and coffee bushes, orange and lime trees, towered over by mango and zapote and mamey trees, all wild trees of the indigenous forest whose fruits are delicious and wholesome."

But Indian Mexico is a long way from Britain, the majority of whose inhabitants are town dwellers with small to medium-sized gardens. I wanted to devise a form of agroforestry tailor-made for our people and climate. Hence the Forest Garden.

The decisive event which made the realisation of this project possible was the advent of Garnet Jones, a countryman of magnificent physique who lives in the village at the bottom of the hill but who originated in the wilds of Mid-Wales. While his whole nature is steeped in traditional country lore and his roots are deep in the soil, he has an alert and lively mind, receptive to new ideas. His enthusiastic participation in the development of the project has been intensely stimulating, while his muscle power has been invaluable. The creation of the Forest Garden has been a partnership between us.

What is a Forest?

Few people in Britain have experienced a real forest. On a private estate not five miles from the centre of the new town of Telford is a tiny relic of the great primaeval forest that once covered almost the whole of South Shropshire. It is the most magical place I know. But no magic exists in the dark regimented ranks of alien conifers which pass for forests in Britain's uplands. They are dead, bereft of atmosphere, of flowers and animals and the infinite variety of form and colour found in the mixed forest. The real forest teems with life.

'The forest is a highly complicated organism, a community of communities'

The mixed forest is the natural climax of ecological development for most parts of the world – if Nature is allowed to unfold its designs without hindrance from man. It is not a mere haphazard conglomeration of plants and animals, but a highly complicated organism, a community of communities, all of whose myriad constituent parts have relationships with each other. Most of these relationships are mutually beneficial though there are also elements of antagonism and competition. Overwhelmingly, the impression one gets is of peace and harmony, so the beneficent forces must far outweigh the antagonistic. In fact, in the forest, as in every healthy living organism, the antagonistic elements, which nature permits in limited 'vaccine' doses to promote resistance to disease and pests, are neutralised.

The interplay of plant and animal activities and processes which leads to the

6 Blackstock Mews, London N4 2BT, UK (rhino@dial.pipex.com), 2003, 27pp, ISBN 0 948826 23 1

neutralising of negative factors and enhancement of positive ones is called 'symbiosis', and its scientific study, which began at least 2,300 years ago with the Greek botanist Theophrastus, is still in its infancy. What is known, however, is that the greater the complexity of the whole – the more plants and animals involved – the greater the energy and fertility generated.

'A particularly rich habitat is provided by the litter of fallen leaves and rotting wood'

The wild life population is accommodated in a wide variety of habitats or 'niches', adapted to different species, from the glade in which roe-deer may be found grazing, or the thicket which may hide a badger's sett, to the clump of nettles or brambles which may be the food-plants of the larvae of several species of moth and butterfly. Each 'storey' provides nesting and roosting places for different species of bird and small mammal. A particularly rich habitat is provided by the litter of fallen leaves and rotting wood found on the forest floor. This provides ideal growing conditions for a number of different fungi, some of which attract insects, while a large number of small creatures can be found boring into the dead wood or sheltering in the moist gloom beneath the litter. In Britain, the most hospitable of all 'hosts' is the English oak, which attracts no fewer than 284 different species of invertebrates.

Beneath the litter are the layers of humus which provide homes for a vast number of living organisms, from microfungi, microflora and microfauna to quite large creatures such as beetles and earthworms. Aristotle showed extraordinary insight into the ecological significance of earthworms when he called them "the intestines of the earth", as they perform the valuable function of grinding coarse soil in their fowl-like gizzards and excreting it, mixed with their digestive juices, in the form of worm-casts. Ceaselessly burrowing and tunnelling to depths that may exceed 14 feet – they never rest or hibernate – earthworms help to open up and maintain the circulation system, by which water, minerals, oxygen and sunlight penetrate into and through the soil.

'The roots of trees and plants are a vast intertwining complex which may extend to thousands of miles'

In a forest the main agents for performing this vital task are the roots of trees and other plants, a vast intertwining complex which may extend to thousands of miles. Impelled by a force capable of splitting rocks, tree roots penetrate deep into the subsoil and through the underlying rockstrata, drawing up minerals and water and making them available to their less deep-rooting neighbours. At the tip of each advancing root-hair is a minute shovel-like cap,

The Forest Garden, £3-50 incl. p&p from Insitute for Social Inventions (tel 020 7359 8391)

made of a tough self-lubricating material, which bores into the earth, at the same time excreting unwanted nutrients which are greedily absorbed by other plants. The tree's roots also continually seek out rocks and stones, which they grip and which afford ever-increasing security of anchorage to the superstructure.

Most soils are more fertile than they appear to be, but elements of fertility tend to be 'locked up' in compacted clods of earth. Where these are broken down and water-borne minerals are free to circulate through the channels and pores of the soil, there is little need for additional fertiliser to be applied; on the forest floor, there is a continuous composting process, as fallen leaves, twigs, blossoms and fruit are mingled with animal droppings.

'Trees act as 'nurses' for less hardy and deep-rooting plants'

The forest's rooting system has a profound effect on the control of water. It maintains the circulation of ground-water and keeps the water-table close to the surface. Trees also act as 'nurses' for less hardy and deep-rooting plants: preparing the soil, supplying moisture, providing shelter from winds and shade from the sun. Leguminous trees and other members of the pea family also benefit neighbouring plants by injecting nitrogen into the soil, with the assistance of friendly bacteria. Another example of symbiosis found in the soil is the 'mycorrhizal association' between trees and certain fungi that habitually grow in forest litter.

There are also many examples of symbiotic relationships between plants and insects. Of special interest to the grower of fruit trees and legumes is the role of insects in pollination, the transfer of pollen-grains, a plant's male cells, to the ovules, or unfertilised seeds, which is essential if a plant is to fruit satisfactorily. Many plants produce brightly coloured and scented blossoms, rich in nectar, to attract bees and other flying insects. In seeking the nectar, the insects get dusted with the pollen, which is brushed off on to the female organs of the next flower they visit. Some plants show a preference for a particular species of insect, forming blossoms that can only be entered by members of that species. The most efficient of all insect-pollinators is the bee, with its hairy legs, to which bundles of pollen can often be seen sticking.

'The first Saxons liked London so little they built their settlements in surrounding forests'

These are but a few examples of the symbiotic process which are well known to science. There can be no doubt that definite proof of many others will be found when scientists seek to confirm or disprove the many traditional associations, especially those involving herbs.

6 Blackstock Mews, London N4 2BT, UK (rhino@dial.pipex.com), 2003, 27pp, ISBN 0 948826 23 1

We all have the forest in our blood. Most of us in Britain have Saxon ancestors who originated in the great forests of South East Germany. When some of the first Saxon colonists to arrive in Britain came upon the thriving market town of post-Roman London, they liked it so little that they bypassed it and built their settlements in clearings which they hewed out of the surrounding forest: Kensington, Islington, Tottenham, Enfield – and Wood Green!

Even when large areas of forest had been cleared to make pastures and cornfields, the Saxons retained woodlands for coppicing and pollarding, to provide timber for building, fencing and tools, fuel for cooking, heating and forging, as well as wild nuts, fruits and herbs for eating and medicine – an early example of Agroforestry.

Luscious Fruits

No epicure dish served at the most expensive restaurant can compare with fresh fruit, organically grown without chemicals and picked from one's own garden. Perhaps the most delicious of all eatables is the true greengage, which is said to have been introduced into Britain from the mountains of Central Asia in ancient times, probably by mediaeval monks. Though a vigorous tree, it seldom crops well, but there are other gages which, while perhaps lacking the 'Oriental' scented flavour of the original wild species, taste almost as good. One of these which I have planted is the Early Transparent Gage, described as 'a connoisseur's fruit of the highest quality'. Another, of which I planted several specimens in my main orchard, is the Denniston's Superb. These have grown into large, hardy, trouble-free trees which seldom fail to give an abundant crop of honey-sweet fruit.

'It should be possible to enjoy one's own outdoor fruit every month of the year'

In many parts of Britain it should be possible, if one has a reasonably large garden, to enjoy one's own outdoor fruit every month of the year, from the first gooseberries, which ripen at the end of May, to the latest apples, which ripen in February and can be stored until June. To extend the picking season as long as possible, one should try to buy at least three varieties – early, mid-season and late – of the fruits of one's choice. This is also desirable in the case of most trees, for the sake of cross-pollination. Almost every fruit tree needs another of a different variety – sometimes two others – for pollination; even those trees that are self-fertile tend to crop better if there are other trees of different varieties in the neighbourhood. Moreover, the complementary trees must blossom at approximately the same time. For successful cropping, therefore, it is most desirable to make a very careful study of the growers' catalogues before buying.

'It is good to have a solid nucleus of hardy fruits that won't let you down'

Like other fruit, plums are divided into categories according to their times of ripening, from July to October. The best flavoured of the earliest is claimed to be a recently introduced variety called Opal, which regularly produces large crops of juicy red-purple fruit. A reliable old variety that is prolific, hardy and has good resistance to frost is Czar, whose black-purple fruit, however, is only considered suitable for cooking. Though I love to experiment with rare and choice fruit, it is good to have a solid nucleus of hardy stand-bys that won't let you down. Another example of these comes in the next time-category, mid-to late August; it is Purple Pershore. The best known of all British plums, Victoria, comes into the same categories of time and reliability, though it is susceptible to silver-leaf disease. The September plums include an epicure variety, Kirke's Blue, which is, however, a light cropper. The latest of all plums is another of my solid stand-bys, Marjorie's Seedling, which can be picked as late as December, provided there are no sharp November frosts. The damsons are also late-ripening and very hardy; when fully ripe, they are surprisingly sweet and can be eaten raw. The two best, which can be grown as hedges, are Farleigh and Shropshire Prune. All plums and damsons, including the 'cookers', are delicious eaten raw if left to stand for an hour or two with a covering of honey.

'Flower of Kent is a falling apple which inspired Newton's Theory of Gravity'

Apples are divided into six categories according to time of ripening. An apple is ready to pick when the stem swells and the fruit comes away after a slight twist. One of the best of the earlies is George Cave, a small crisp apple that crops well and is sometimes ready before the end of July. Moving on to early October, I find my Spartans have a wine-rich flavour that matches their purple hue – far superior to shop Spartans. Slightly later is my favourite apple, Sunset, a small, crisp apple from the Cox stable, hardier and, to my mind, even more fragrant than its more famous relative. Later still are two recent introductions from East Malling, the finest fruit-breeding station in the world. They are Jupiter and Suntan, a cross between Cox and Court Pendu Plat, which may be the oldest of all apples, dating back to Roman times. Another old apple, dating back at least to 1720, is Ashmead's Kernel, a russet type that was once voted the best of all apples for flavour. A late cooker is Flower of Kent, a falling apple which inspired Isaac Newton to conceive the Theory of Gravity.

6 Blackstock Mews, London N4 2BT, UK (rhino@dial.pipex.com), 2003, 27pp, ISBN 0 948826 23 1

Possibly the best keeper of all is another cooking apple, Annie Elizabeth, which can be stored until June.

Pears can be divided into two main categories: the richly scented, juicy but rather delicate French epicure varieties, such as Jargonelle and Doyenne du Comice, and the more down-to-earth English varieties such as Improved Fertility, Hessle and Conference. A small Improved Fertility is one of my favourite 'Old Reliables'. It has never failed, for 30 years, to give a bumper crop of small, sweet fruit, with a rough texture which rather appeals to me, although it is boxed in with red, white and black currants – one of the facts that inspired me to conceive the Forest Garden.

'Along the fence are fan-trained plums interplanted with blackcurrants'

All bush and cane fruits, except blueberries, are suitable for the Forest Garden, because all will tolerate some shade. Along the fence above the Packhorse Track are fan-trained plums interplanted with blackcurrants. Along a short mound is a hedge of Ben Sarek blackcurrants, a new introduction by the Scottish Crop Research Institute. They produce fruit as large and sweet as grapes. From the same Institute comes a mid-season raspberry, Glen Cova. Next to it is the very latest in autumn-fruiting raspberries, which form compact bushes which don't need staking. It is Autumn Bliss, a hybrid produced by East Malling – after years of endless patience – combining an Arctic raspberry, the American wild raspberry and no fewer than six old British varieties.

Among the hybrid berries I am trying are the Japanese Wineberry, the Japanese Strawberry-Raspberry and the Boysenberry. Once believed to be a blackcurrant-gooseberry hybrid, the Worcesterberry, which I am also growing, is in fact a wild American gooseberry; its deliciously sweet small berries are deep purple, almost black. Among gooseberries that are particularly suitable for the Forest Garden, on account of their shade-tolerance, are Whinham's Industry, which also produces a purple berry. Wild and Alpine strawberries also fit very well into the Forest Garden, as they too flourish in shady conditions.

'Growers' catalogues enumerate mouthwatering varieties of peach, nectarine, apricot'

There are many other delicious fruits which can be grown out-of-doors in many parts of Britain, but which, alas, are not suitable for this exposed chilly hillside. Growers' catalogues enumerate mouthwatering varieties of peach, nectarine, apricot, cherry, fig and almond trees as well as kiwi fruits and grapes.

The nuts I grow are Kentish cobs, filberts, a sweet chestnut and a walnut of a new German variety called Bucca neer, which is said to come into bearing sooner than the English walnut. I also grow black and white mulberries, and a 'sweet rowan', a honey locust with edible beans and a bamboo, which I hope will produce edible shoots in the spring.

Fragrant Herbs, Spicy Vegetables

'The salad, the most nourishing of all dishes, has enormous scope for expansion'

Our forefathers made no distinction between vegetables and herbs. Anything that was edible and green, cultivated or wild, was liable to be included in their 'sallets'. John Evelyn in his *Acetaria*, the classic work on 'sallets' published in 1699, enumerates 73 plants that were commonly eaten raw in his day, and adds that many more could have been included. Even today several plants are on the borderline between being regarded as vegetables or herbs. Is lovage, that magnificent perennial relative of celery that can grow to a height of eight feet, a vegetable or a herb? There is similar doubt about fennel and sorrel. Does it matter anyhow? What does matter is that the salad, the most nourishing of all dishes which everyone ought to enjoy every day, has enormous scope for expansion.

'More than 140 plants are suitable for salads'

Joy Larkcom, John Evelyn's illustrious present-day successor, shows the way in her fascinating book *The Salad Garden* (Windward, London, 1984), in which she enumerates more than 140 plants as being suitable for salads. In a tour of the continent she discovered that many of Evelyn's 'sallet' plants were still being eaten in countries from Portugal to Hungary, and also came across a number that Evelyn was unaware of. Later she added to her collection many Oriental plants that are now becoming available through English seedsmen.

Of Joy Larkcom's plants at least a third are suitable for a Forest Garden, in which herbaceous plants must be limited to three categories: those that are perennial or that readily self-seed, plus a number of root vegetables, so that the rhizosphere can be utilised.

Of the perennial vegetables that Joy discovered, the most remarkable are a large number of different types of chicory that she found being cultivated in various regions of Italy. Some are very decorative. My favourite is Treviso, which starts out green but transforms itself in the autumn into a pyramid of crimson, sharply pointed leaves. Unlike some chicories, which can be coarse

6 Blackstock Mews, London N4 2BT, UK (rhino@dial.pipex.com), 2003, 27pp, ISBN 0 948826 23 1

and bitter, the inner leaves of Treviso are mild and tender, while looking very pretty in a salad. Probably the hardiest is Grumolo, a bottle-green chicory from the mountains of Piedmont. Through the winter it hugs the ground as a tight rosette, but later forms a tall, narrow pagoda. The wild chicory or 'succory' tastes and looks like a dandelion – until it blooms, when, like all chicories, it produces exquisite sky-blue flowers. It has edible roots.

Another very useful hardy perennial is sorrel, a kind of wild spinach whose leaves have a delightful lemon flavour. French sorrel has large leaves, while Buckler-leaved sorrel, as its name implies, has small leaves shaped like heraldic shields; it is a useful spreading plant for the 'ground-storey'. Related to sorrel and equally hardy is Good King Henry, sometimes flatteringly known as 'Lincolnshire asparagus'.

'Several perennial onions act as an effective screen against rabbits'

A plant with jade green, spinach-shaped leaves and white flowers like lilies-of-the-valley is wild garlic or 'ramsons'. The leaves have much of the true garlic flavour, though sweeter and milder than the bulbs, and, for those who like that flavour, are among the most crisp and delicious of salad vegetables. There are also several perennial onions which are very suitable for the borders of the Forest Garden – where they are said to act as an effective screen against rabbits. These include chives, Chinese garlic chives, 'Welsh' onions, which in fact come from Siberia, and 'tree' onions, which form tiny bulbs at the tops of their stalks. A very decorative perennial vegetable is the cardoon, a thistle relative of the globe artichoke, which is also perennial.

There is little or no room in the Forest Garden for brassicas, which, besides being annuals, are greedy feeders and bad neighbours, taking a lot of fertility out of the soil and giving very little back. A possible exception is Nine-Star broccoli, which is perennial. Among useful self-seeding vegetables, with a notable spicy flavour, are land cress and Italian rocket.

The most suitable root vegetables are Hamburg Parsley, which tolerates shade, red radishes, which do best in shade if sown late, and the very hardy black Spanish and purple French winter radishes, which come into their own when the members of the herbaceous layer die down.

'Herbs have a symbiotic effect on other plants, stimulating them and warding off pests'

Herbs, of course, are not only suitable for eating, but also have medicinal value and are credited with remarkable symbiotic effects on other plants, stimulating them and warding off pests and disease germs. The herbs most suited for a Forest Garden are those which are said to be beneficial to fruit trees, which include tansy, southernwood and pennyroyal. I train nasturtiums up the apple trees, because they are believed to deter woolly aphis.

My favourite herb is lemon-balm, whose leaves give a delicious fragrance to fruit-salads. Throughout history tremendous claims have been made for its potency. It is said to 'radiate a beneficent atmosphere' on neighbouring plants and an old rhyme goes so far as to claim that

'If you eat balm every day,

You will live for aye.'

John Evelyn describes 'baum' as 'cordial and exhilarating' and claims that it is 'sovereign for the Brain, strengthening the Memory, and powerfully chasing away Melancholy.'

Next to balm I love the mints, with their wide range of scents and flavours: applemint, pineapplemint, peppermint, spearmint, ginger mint, lemon mint, water mint, curly mint, Korean mint, calamint and above all, eau-de-cologne mint, which John Evelyn and the Americans call orangemint, and which I'm inclined to think has the most delicious fragrance in Nature. The mints are said to be particularly effective in deterring pests; peppermint is even said to deter rats and mice. Evelyn describes spearmint as 'friendly to the weak Stomach, and powerful against all Nervous Crudities.'

Among many other herbs that are suitable for the Forest Garden are sweet cicely, marjoram, sage and bergamot, with its lovely uncommon crimson flowers.

Design and Maintenance

The oldest inhabitant of my Forest Garden is an ancient twisted damson with triple trunk, up which I have trained a Brant vine. It stands guard over the entrance, opposite the greenhouse and the toolshed, which was once the privy. It was almost definitely planted by 'Boney' Higgins, a former tenant of the farm and famous local character, who died in 1947, just before his 100th birthday. 'Boney' was a mighty wielder of the scythe and saw, and also a mighty consumer of cider made by his nephew, who was an itinerant cider-maker like the hero of Hardy's novel *The Woodlanders.*

'One's criteria should be aesthetic, inspirational, rather than utilitarian'

Many gardens already have one or two fruit or nut trees that can constitute the focal point, the nucleus, of a Forest Garden design. One can begin with a framework of standard fruit trees at recommended intervals, then fill in the gaps with dwarf trees, currants and gooseberries, with herb and perennial vegetable plants (available from herb farms) beneath. Every Forest Garden

6 Blackstock Mews, London N4 2BT, UK (rhino@dial.pipex.com), 2003, 27pp, ISBN 0 948826 23 1

should be different, growing naturally out of its environment. One should forget about the rigid lines of conventional orchards and kitchen gardens and think in terms of the natural forest; one's criteria should be aesthetic, inspirational, rather than utilitarian. What looks right for the plants should be best for the development of the whole.

'It is a good idea to build mounds so that plants can be grown both on top and on the sides'

To give a more natural look to the landscape, and also to economise space, it is a good idea to build one or two mounds, about three feet high, with flat tops and sloping sides so that plants can be grown both on top and on the sides. The best procedure is to begin by digging a one-foot deep trench, which should be filled with coarse plant-material, such as small branches, hedge cuttings, currant prunings and sunflower stalks. This core, which should be as loose as possible to allow for a free flow of air and water, should be covered with sods, grass-side downwards. Then should follow a layer of dead weeds and other vegetable residues, covered with compost or well rotted manure and lime. Finally the mound needs to be topped with soil.

Where hedges or fences are needed, these should comprise or incorporate fruit or nut trees, bushes or climbers. The simplest hedge consists of dwarf pyramid fruit or nut trees planted at three and a half foot intervals, or blackcurrant bushes planted at one foot intervals, and allowed to grow into each other. Under the French Bouche-Thomas system, the trees are planted diagonally for mutual support. Alternatively, one can erect lattice fences to which are attached fan-trained plums or peaches or cordon or espalier apples, pears, cherries or nuts. It should be remembered, however, that these are far less productive than free-growing trees. Again, one can train raspberries, blackberries or hybrid berries, such as the Boysenberry, Japanese Wineberry or Tayberry, up ordinary fences. Another possibility is to plant an old-fashioned farm-hedge of mixed trees and shrubs, such as elders, hazels, damsons, bullaces and crabapples.

'The very essence of the Forest Garden concept is diversity'

The very essence of the Forest Garden concept is diversity. As wide a range as possible of different species and varieties of fruit, nuts, vegetables and herbs should be planted. In the first year I planted in my small area more than 100 species and varieties. Some of these die, others spread, occupying more and more space, but I intend to keep the total number as high as possible, filling gaps with bought plants or cuttings raised in my small tree nursery.

Once a year, when the herbaceous plants die down in the late autumn, a deep layer of compost or straw is spread throughout the garden, to protect roots from frost and to suppress spring weeds. With adequate mulching, plants tend to grow freely and suppress competitors themselves. However, I periodically find it necessary, especially after rain when weeds can readily be pulled up by the roots, to embark on a 'crawl-and-claw' expedition through the undergrowth. Armed with a stout pair of gardening gloves, the most tenacious weeds can be clawed out from the interstices of valued plants. The fragrance of the ever-present herbs makes this an enjoyable and satisfying task.

Weeding loses most of its daunting prospect as a backbreaking chore if carried out as a regular routine in connection with other work. During twice-daily picking sessions, when fruit, vegetables and herbs are gathered fresh for meals, I pull up most of the more obtrusive weeds in my path, adding them to the mulch. Picking is part of the process of pruning surplus growth and cutting back plants that encroach on their neighbours.

Adjuncts to Forest Garden

The Forest Garden also has two adjuncts:

1 *The Ante(i)-Forest Garden*, so called because it came before the Forest Garden in time and comes before it in space (ante), and also because it contains plants that are antagonistic to Forest Garden shade and soil (anti).

2. *The John Evelyn Arboretum*: a collection of specimen trees, including some rare species, that are suitable for temperate agroforestry schemes. The arboretum also includes a pond, an osier coppice, cut annually for basketry, a bog-garden irrigated by waterwheel, a reed-bed, a wildlife reserve, and an 'energy plantation' of willows, coppiced and shredded for fuel and compost.

The Ante(i)-Forest Garden

In a corner near the gate is Where It All Began: my first experiment in plant symbiosis or companion planting. It comprises a small Improved Fertility Pear, surrounded by red, white and black currants and herbs. A tiny area, yet intensely productive, year after year.

'Beds for those plants which require full sunlight and special soils'

At the other side of the gate is the Patio Garden, a mini-forest-garden designed for the person who has no garden but only a paved yard with room for tubs and a trellis for climbers. It mainly comprises a number of tubs containing lime-hating plants in ericacious compost: blueberries and a witch hazel, as well as two dwarf apples, a berberis, herbs in pots and climbing and

6 Blackstock Mews, London N4 2BT, UK (rhino@dial.pipex.com), 2003, 27pp, ISBN 0 948826 23 1

trailing strawberries.

Now we come to the 'Anti' beds: those for plants which require full sunlight and special soils. One comprises herbs such as thyme, yarrow and rue, which thrive in peat. The other is a miniature bog garden, its soil, again mainly peat, spread above a plastic sheet such as is used for making ponds. It comprises cranberries, whortleberries and blueberries.

Though there is a seedbed for annual vegetables and other beds for planting them out – largely Continental and Oriental salad plants – the Anti-Forest-Garden mainly comprises perennials, including asparagus, seakale and chicory.

The John Evelyn Arboretum

Entered through the wrought-iron Arch of Gaia, the Arboretum includes trees from every continent, from Africa (an Atlas Cedar) to the Far North (a Silver Birch) and the Far South (Nothofagus antartica, the Southern Beech, which grows in Tierra del Fuego and on the southern tip of New Zealand).

'The only tree which experiences a masochistic pleasure in having its bark torn to shreds'

The Southern Beech is the fastest-growing of all non-tropical, broad-leaved timber trees. Another of the many fascinating trees is a small Shagbark Hickory, valuable both for its very hard timber and for its nuts. It is the native tree of the grey squirrel in North America – the only tree which actually experiences a masochistic pleasure in having its bark torn to shreds. Other North American trees include a Sugar Maple, a Balsam Poplar, with exquisite scent, a Red Oak, a Scarlet Oak and a rare Rose Oak. Other nut trees include a German Walnut, a French Chestnut, an Arolla Pine and a small hedge of assorted Hazels, including two purple varieties and Corylus contorta, 'Harry Lauder's Walking Stick'.

Two English native trees which produce edible fruit are a Whitebeam and a rare Wild Service tree. Also fruit-bearers are two Mulberries, one Black – the best for eating – and the other White – the variety used for silkworm production. There are also two ornamental Crabs, with beautiful purple foliage, and a red Japanese Maple. Conifers include a Swedish Juniper, a Scots Pine, a Giant Fir and a Western Red Cedar, used by the Indians of British Columbia for making totem-poles and ocean-going canoes. A plastic tunnel houses two Kiwi Fruits or Chinese Gooseberries – male and female, otherwise there would be no fruit.

On the south-west side of the Arboretum, with a beautiful view over a cornfield, stands 'Cookery Nook', a small ecological house, cleverly designed and built from local timber by my partner Garnet Jones. It houses a small, primitive but efficient cast-iron stove ('Topsy'), which once graced the brake-van of an old-fashioned goods train; on this I do my cooking. At the back of Cookery Nook is a lean-to ecological lavatory, which contains a bucket of straw underneath the seat, from which protrudes, at the time of writing, an inquisitive hogweed. After use, the contents of the bucket are sprinkled with lime and emptied on to the neighbouring compost heap, which will be used for non-food trees.

Electric lighting is provided by a wind-generator ('Winnie-the-Pooh') sited opposite a gap in the hedge to take full advantage of the predominant south-west wind, as it blows up Apedale. Fuel for Topsy comes largely from our own hedgerows, prunings and rotten stakes, so Cookery Nook is mainly self-sufficient in lighting and heating.

'Sallets' for Positive Health

'Make food your medicine and medicine your food'. So wrote Hippocrates, the Father of Medicine, and our classically educated forefathers of the 16th and 17th centuries must have been familiar with his words: a standard article of their diet was a 'sallet' or 'salmagundy' comprising a wide variety of cultivated and wild fruit, vegetables and herbs. The popular herbalists of the time had made them fully aware of the health-promoting qualities of the ingredients. In view of the research carried out during the last century by such pioneer nutritionists as Bircher-Benner into the effects on the human body and mind of raw, fresh, organically grown foods, it is not surprising that 16th and 17th century England saw a remarkable flowering of creativity in literature, science, religion, political theory, music, education, exploration and medicine.

'Men and women are what they eat and drink – and think'

Men and women are what they eat and drink – and think. All our most delicate and complicated organs, including the brain, heart, glands, nervous system, liver etc, are made of the food and beverages that we ingest and that are distributed throughout our bodies by the blood. Therefore, the quality of the blood is of prime importance for health. The best of all blood-foods is one of the world's most wonderful substances: chlorophyll. This is the green pigment in plants which, by the process of photosynthesis, has the unique ability to create living matter by harnessing the power of the sun, a process which lies at the heart of all physical life. The chemical composition of chlorophyll is almost identical to that of human blood, and its value as nourishment and as a remedy for blood disorders, such as high blood-

6 Blackstock Mews, London N4 2BT, UK (rhino@dial.pipex.com), 2003, 27pp, ISBN 0 948826 23 1

pressure, has been amply demonstrated. But the value of chlorophyll is reduced by cooking and preservation. Therefore, in the opinion of Bircher-Benner and other nutritionists, the single most important factor in diet must be the raw green leaf.

Another basic necessity for good blood is an abundance of iron, which is the main constituent of the red cells. Among the best sources of iron is fresh fruit, such as apples, plums and pears, as well as nuts and onions. Fresh fruit, above all blackcurrants, is also one of the best sources of Vitamin C, which is primarily concerned with building up the body's immune system, thereby protecting us from disease. Vitamin C is easily destroyed by cooking and other forms of processing, and, unlike other vitamins, it is not stored or manufactured within the body's tissues. Therefore, to maintain a reliable, lasting state of health, it is essential to replenish our stocks of Vitamin C every day. This is best done by daily consumption of fresh, raw fruit and vegetables.

'Many plants contain the precise enzymes that are necessary to digest them'

The motive-power for many of the body's highly complicated mechanisms is provided by the enzymes: tiny, highly specialised chemical catalysts that exist in every cell. They perform the extraordinary feat of transforming the food we eat into entirely different substances, such as blood, bones, hair and fingernails – a feat that human ingenuity is incapable of duplicating. They are also at the heart of every chemical action in the body: including those involved in growth, nerve-impulses and the movements of muscles. While some enzymes are manufactured by the body, most are derived from minerals in the food we eat, including iron, potassium, manganese, copper and zinc. The best sources of these and other minerals are deep-rooting plants which draw them from the subsoil. We also imbibe complete enzymes from plant cells and it is an interesting fact that many plants contain the precise enzymes that are necessary to digest them.

'The mineral-richness of herbs is largely responsible for their traditional healing virtues'

Many herbs are deep-rooting perennials and there is no doubt that their mineral-richness is largely responsible for their traditional healing virtues. Modern research confirms that plants contain many marvellous substances as well as minerals that have healing power and are incorporated in drugs. These include alkaloids which affect the nervous system, bitter principles which promote digestion and other metabolic functions, essential oils, which are anti-inflammatory, flavonoids, which are used for the treatment of heart troubles, ulcers and arthritis, glycosides which are anti-spasmodics, mucilages which are used for constipation and chest troubles and tannins, which are widely incorporated in remedies for dysentery and slow-healing wounds.

Prevention is better than cure, and there is no doubt that if one includes in one's diet a wide variety of herbs and other plants containing these substances, one's heart, lungs, nerves, eyes, and other vital organs are strengthened, so that the need for medical treatment is avoided.

'A diet mainly consisting of raw foods is the best way of achieving a state of wholeness'

Health is not mere absence of disease but, in the words of Leslie and Susannah Kenton in *Raw Energy* (Century, London, 1984), it is 'a dynamic state of mind and body that makes it possible for you to participate in the fullness of life'.

The authors quote research by many leading scientists and physicians which confirms their thesis that a diet mainly consisting of raw foods is the best way of achieving a state of wholeness and resistance to infection. But there is no need to allow worry about scientific considerations to spoil the sheer pleasure of enjoying the many delicious recipes that they and Joy Larkcom give. If one eats a wide variety of fresh fruit and vegetables and fresh or dried herbs every day, it is reasonably certain that these will include all the nutritional factors the body needs. Flavour is an indication of nutrient content, and one interesting aspect of the raw food experience is the gradual reawakening of the basic nutritional instinct which man naturally shares with wild animals. One's palate learns to detect the subtle qualities that distinguish fresh, organically grown food from processed food and one instinctively rejects toxins before they have time to build up in the system and cause trouble.

Having enjoyed the mainly raw diet for over ten years, I can testify to its efficacy in building up and releasing the potential that exist in all human systems, above all the mental qualities of alertness, will-power and creativity.

6 Blackstock Mews, London N4 2BT, UK (rhino@dial.pipex.com), 2003, 27pp, ISBN 0 948826 23 1

Recommended suppliers

• Chris Bowers and Sons, 'Whispering Trees', Wimbotsham, Norfolk PE24 8QB (tel 01366 388752). Suppliers of fruit, nut and ornamental trees and bushes, soft fruit and asparagus.

• Chiltern Seeds, Bortree Stile, Ulverston, Cumbria LA12 7PB (tel 01229 581137; e-mail: info@chilternseeds.co.uk; web: www.chilternseeds.co.uk). Suppliers of a huge range of annual, perennial, and uncommon vegetable, herb, tree and shrub seeds.

• Deacon's Nursery, Godshill, Isle of Wight PO38 3HW (tel 01983 840750). Supply fruit trees and bushes, 'family' trees.

• Harley Nurseries, between Much Wenlock and Cressage, Shropshire (tel 01952 510241). Suppliers of fruit and ornamental trees and bushes (not mail order).

• Highfield Nurseries, Whitminster, nr Gloucester GL2 7PL (tel 01452 741309/740266; e-mail: highfield.gs@freeuk.com). Suppliers of trees, fruit trees and bushes.

• Hillier Nurseries, Ampfield House, nr Romsey, Hants S051 9PA (tel 01794 368 733). Supply a large selection of trees and shrubs (no mail order).

• S.E. Marshalls and Co, 'Marshalls Seeds', Wisbech, Cambs PE132RF (tel 01945 583407; web: www.marshalls-seeds.co.uk). Suppliers of perennial vegetable and soft fruit seeds.

• Ken Muir, Weeley Heath, Clacton-on-Sea, Essex CO16 9BJ (tel 01255 830181; e-mail: info@kenmuir.co.uk; web: www.kenmuir.co.uk). Fruit specialists who supply a full range of miniature fruit and nut trees, ornamental trees, and soft fruit canes.

• Scott's Nurseries, Merriott, Somerset TA16 5PL (tel 01460 72306). Suppliers of fruit, nut and ornamental trees and bushes, and perennial plants.

• Suffolk Herbs, Little Cornard, nr Sudbury, Suffolk CO10 ONY (tel 01376 572456; e-mail: sales@suffolkherbs.com; web: www.suffolkherbs.com). Suppliers of herbs and uncommon vegetable seeds.

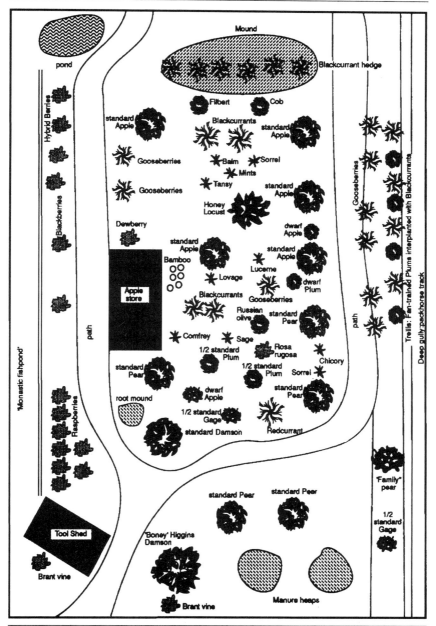

Mound

pond

Blackcurrant hedge

Hybrid Berries

Filbert

Cob

standard Apple

Blackcurrants

standard Apple

Goosebaries

Balm

Sorrel

Mints

Blackberries

Goosaberries

Tansy

standard Apple

Honey Locust

Goosebaries

Dewberry

dwarf Apple

standard Apple

standard Apple

Bamboo

Lovage

Lucerne

dwarf Plum

Apple store

Blackcurrants

Goosaberries

Russian olive

standard Pear

path

"Monastic fishpond"

Comfrey

Sage

Rosa rugosa

1/2 standard Plum

1/2 standard Plum

Chicory

standard Pear

Sorrel

standard Pear

Raspberries

root mound

dwarf Apple

standard Pear

1/2 standard Gage

standard Damson

Redcurrant

Trellis: Fan-trained Plums interplanted with Blackcurrants

path

Deep gully:packhorse track

"Family" pear

1/2 standard Gage

Tool Shed

standard Pear

standard Pear

Brant vine

"Boney" Higgins Damson

Brant vine

Manure heaps

6 Blackstock Mews, London N4 2BT, UK (rhino@dial.pipex.com), 2003, 27pp, ISBN 0 948826 23 1

The Institute for Social Inventions is a project of the Nicholas Albery Foundation which launches good ideas for improving the quality of life. It launched and helps administer and shares an office with The Natural Death Centre. It offers subscriptions and publications. Please tick which of the following apply:

• **I wish to be sent the following PUBLICATIONS** - (p&p included. 10% off for Institute subscribers, except for those books marked [*]

[*] **The New Natural Death Handbook**, 3rd ed, expensive green and DIY funerals, 180+ woodland burial grounds, cardboard coffins, Good Funeral Guide to undertakers, caring for the dying at home, living wills, 382 pp. £12-99 incl. p&p & update sheets (£13-50 1st class by credit card, by phone or on the web: www.naturaldeath.org.uk)

[*] **How to Organise a Woodland or Inexpensive Funeral.** For a credit card phone or web donation of £6-99, this summary (less detailed than the Handbook above) can be e-mailed to those with e-mail and web access who are in urgent need. It is only available as an e-mail.

[*] **Living Will & set of forms** including Life Values Statement, Death Plan, Advance Funeral Wishes. Set of forms for a donation of £5 or more.

[*] **Progressive Endings,** changing attitudes to death, dying and funerals. Complements the New Natural Death Handbook. £6-20 incl. 1st class p&p.

[*] **Ways to go – Naturally** complements the Handbook and is for all those interested in the woodland burial and natural death movements. £6-20 incl. 1st class p&p.

[*] **Poem for the Day – 366 Poems, Old and New, Worth Learning By Heart**, with foreword by Wendy Cope. 400 page book with a poem for each day of the year and Poetry Challenges. £11-97 incl. p&p.

[*] **Seize the Day – A Calendar of Tips for Living from 366 Extraordinary People,** with foreword by Anita Roddick and introduction by Brian Eno. 384 pp. £13-99 incl. p&p.

[*] **Time Out Book of Country Walks**, the new blue-cover, revised edition of the 416-page calendar of walks easily reached by train as day outings from London, with a pub at lunchtime and a tea place afterwards. £11-99 (incl. update sheets, train times for Saturday Walkers' Club, p&p).

• **Book of Inspirations – A directory of social inventions,** prefaces by Brian Eno and Nicholas Albery. £15 incl. p&p.

• **Cornucopia – A global ideas bank compendium,** prefaces by Brian Eno and the late Nicholas Albery. £15 incl. p&p.

• **Social Dreams and Technological Nightmares – A global ideas bank compendium** predicting the next 500 years, £14-85 incl. p&p.

• **DIY Futures – People's ideas and projects for a better world,** 250 new social incentives, £14-85 incl. p&p.

FOR THE ABOVE FOUR IDEAS BOOKS, ONE COSTS **£15**, TWO COST **£25**, THREE COST **£30** AND FOUR COST **£36** PLEASE TICK WHICH ONES YOU WANT.

• **The World's Greatest Ideas,** a "best of" compendium of the Institute's work from the past ten years: a veritable feast of ideas. £15 inc p&p.

• **1,001 Health Tips – from recent medical research,** £6-99 or **FREE!** to *new* Institute subscribers. Get well and stay well.

• **Alternative Gomera** guide to a fortnight's walking round Gomera Island near Tenerife by Nicholas Albery, 7th edition with town maps. £11 incl. p&p. Map £5-85 extra.

• **How to Feel Reborn? Varieties of Rebirthing Experiences**, a 260 page investigation of primal and rebirthing therapies by Nicholas Albery. The 1985 edition, now available in digital version which you can download and print out, £9-99. Go to www.globalideasbank.org/rebirthing.html for free chapter and ordering details.

• The book **Community Counselling Circles** by John Southgate, for improving the atmosphere in groups, £6-95.

• **The Solution for South Africa**, influential cantonisation scheme, £6-95.

• **Future Workshops – How to Create Desirable Futures**, by Robert Jungk, used by groups throughout Europe as a manual, £8-99.

• **The Problem Solving Pocketbook**, an overview of all the main ways to solve problems, plus some wild ones, £3-50.

• **Being True to Yourself** by Margaret Chisman, insight exercises for groups, by Margaret Chisman. £4-95.

• **Auction of Promises – How to raise £16,000 in one evening**, for church, school and community groups. £1-95.

• The original Institute **Journals** from the 1980s. £10 for a random five issues.

INSTITUTE SUBSCRIPTIONS

• Enclosed is £15 for an Institute **subscription**. (Outside UK £17 by credit card).

(£1 off above £15 fee for those who pay by UK Standing Order. For standing order instructions: state your bank's name, address and your account number, the annual payment, date to start and our bank and account details as below. Include your name, address, tel number and signature.) Subscribers receive the annual book-length Annual in the summer – *state if you want this year's or next year's* – and get as a bonus another Institute book – currently '1,001 Health Tips' – plus 10 % off most Institute publications, except those with [*]. They can also receive occasional e-mailings informing them about Insitute events and ideas.

Outside UK:
• p&p: add 9% to total for surface mail; 32 % airmail.

Outside UK, you must pay one of these ways:

• by UK bank or by UK cash notes.

• By UK sterling by bankers draft **with bank charges paid your end**: (to Institute for Social Inventions account, bank number 60 13 34, account number 38843803, bank address: National Westminster Bank, 298 Elgin Avenue, London W9, UK).

• By credit card: please add 4.2% for bank's credit card fee. We accept non-Switch cards: MasterCard or Visa. Give your cardholder number, expiry date, registered address, name and initials & signature (or phone, fax, e-mail or pay secure online at w w w . g l o b a l i d e a s b a n k . o r g / bookorder.html). This is the cheapest way to pay from outside the UK.

Please return this form with your name and address and cheques payable to: **Institute for Social Inventions**, 6 Blackstock Mews, London N4 2BT, (tel 020 7359 8391; fax 020 7354 3831; e-mail: rhino@dial.pipex.com).

6 Blackstock Mews, London N4 2BT, UK (rhino@dial.pipex.com), 2003, 27pp, ISBN 0 948826 23 1